Christmas
STICKER BOOK

By Susannah Bradley
Illustrated by Victor Ambrus

You can retell the Christmas story with the colour pages in this book. In the centre you will find stickers that can be used on the coloured backgrounds. There are three scenes depicting the shepherds in the fields, the stable in Bethlehem and the three kings following the star. Keep the stickers on their backing page when you are not using them so that you can use them again and again. Use crayons or felt tip pens to colour all the other lovely pictures of Christmas time, and read about the traditions of Christmas and about the way it is celebrated in other lands.

British Library Cataloguing in Publication Data
Bradley, Susannah
Christmas sticker book.
1. Christmas—Juvenile literature
I. Title II. Ambrus, Victor
394.2'68282 GT4985

ISBN 0-361-07406-9

Published 1986 by Purnell Books
a division of Macdonald & Co (Publishers) Ltd
Greater London House, Hampstead Road, London NW1 7QX
a BPCC plc company
Reprinted 1987, 1988

First published 1983 by Purnell Books
exclusively for Marks and Spencer plc

Christmas Customs

Happy Christmas, everybody! Every year on December 25th Christians throughout the world celebrate the birth of Jesus Christ. But no one knows exactly when he was born. It was the Romans who fixed the date in AD 336. It suited them to celebrate the Christmas festival then, because it fell in the middle of an old pagan feasting time, when they celebrated the god, Saturn. As Christians they no longer worshipped Saturn, but they still liked to feast.

Nowadays Christmas conjures up thoughts of holly berries heavy on the boughs, snowy scenes (usually only on Christmas cards!), fairy lights on Christmas trees, stockings hung up by the bed and mince pies left for Father Christmas.

Father Christmas, or Santa Claus, is based on St. Nicholas, who was Bishop of Myra in Turkey. He probably didn't look much like our Father Christmas with his red tunic and high knee boots — and I'm sure he didn't ride through the sky with his reindeer, but he had the same reputation for kindness and generosity.

Christmas Customs

Christmas is such a time for tradition that we tend to do the same things every year without stopping to wonder how the customs came to be. So let's look at a few of them, and see how they have developed through the ages.

Many of the customs existed before people celebrated Christmas. The pagans, as we call people who lived before the Christians and worshipped many gods, had feasts and celebrations long before Christ was born and they had customs to go with them. Pagan gods included the Sun and the Moon, although they were given different

The Christmas Tree

Before the Romans became Christians they decorated trees with small gifts at feast times. The Egyptians used palm branches for decoration. Christmas trees decorated with candles were to be found in German homes, but Britain did not introduce them into its celebrations until Prince Albert, Queen Victoria's German husband, introduced the custom at Windsor.

Our most famous Christmas tree stands in Trafalgar Square, ablaze with light. It is an annual gift from the people of Norway to the people of Britain for help given in World War II.

But why an evergreen tree? That's another hangover from pagan times. People believed that woodland spirits lived inside the evergreens!

names in different countries. When Christianity came the well-loved customs were adapted to the new Christian celebration.

Mistletoe

Before Christian times the mistletoe was a sacred plant to the pagan priests known as Druids — so important to them that even today it is not allowed inside many Christian churches.

There is a legend about the plant that says it was a sturdy tree until it was used to make the Cross for Christ's crucifixion. Afterwards it was so disgraced by this that it ceased to have a life of its own, but was forced to live as a parasite on the branches of other trees.

On the lighter side of things it has earned itself the meaning 'Give me a kiss' in the language of flowers — and we hang it up over doorways so that anyone passing under it may be kissed. For each kiss a berry should be removed from the mistletoe — and, when all the berries have been plucked, that's an end to the kissing!

Christmas Cards

Around the middle of the nineteenth century, people in Britain began to send seasonal cards to each other at the end of December. But they were not Christmas cards. They were sent to wish their friends and relatives a very happy new year — and it was another forty years or so before Christmas wishes were included, too.

So the custom began as 'posting late for Christmas'!

The Yule Log

If any one Christmas custom is dying out, this is it — because so many homes no longer have open fires and the Yule log can't be burnt with all the ceremony that has come down with it through the years.

It began in pagan times, when the burning of a log symbolised the fire and heat that the people worshipped. You may no longer find a Yule log in your fireplace, but look for it on your table. Could your Yule log be nestling there — a disguised swiss roll?

The Christmas Stocking

Do you hang up a stocking, or are you one of the greedy ones who hang up a pillowcase?

No, that's not quite fair. People who hang up a pillowcase often find *all* their presents inside it, while the stocking-hangers usually find larger presents under the tree, later on.

But why a stocking? After all, it's a strange shape to put things in . . .

The legend says that dear old St. Nicholas once gave gifts to the three daughters of a ruined businessman. He threw some bags of gold into their house, and they happened to fall into a stocking which was drying by the fire. So the stocking became the very thing to hold a present or two from Father Christmas.

Food

We all think of turkey as the traditional Christmas dinner, but it is a custom imported from America. Before the English discovered turkey they ate roast goose at Christmas. Go back a few centuries more and you might have served a boar's head, or roast peacock.

Mince pies have changed over the centuries. In the Middle Ages they contained chopped meat instead of the sweet filling they have now. They were rectangular and had a small pastry baby on the crust, to represent the Christ Child in the manger. The Puritans put a stop to that in the seventeenth century, saying that it was wicked to show such images of Christ. But if you wanted to renew the custom, you could try your hand at a few pastry babies next baking day!

Baboushka's Story

There are Christmas legends from every country in Christendom — and this one, from Russia, is one of the most famous of all. Baboushka means Grandmother, and she learned her lesson the hard way . . .

My cottage in old Russia stood,
Quite isolated, in a wood.
I always kept it spick and span,
As well as an old woman can,
And made a palace of my home
Not dreaming I would ever roam;
I little knew what lay in store
When strangers knocked upon my door.

There were but three, and richly dressed,
They asked for shelter, food and rest.
I showed them in, and while they dined
I asked them what they'd come to find.
"A king!" they said. "Much farther on,
A babe to feast your eyes upon."
"Can I come with you, please?" I cried.
"I'm old, but I can surely ride."

"We leave tonight," the wise men said.
And so I sent them on ahead.
Well, really! How could I walk out,
Leaving the washing-up about?
Next day, with presents in my packs
I set my donkey in their tracks.
A star was guiding them, I knew;
All right — then it could guide me, too!

Alas — the stars all looked the same!
I only had myself to blame.
I should have taken my big chance
And left without a backward glance.
Since then I've travelled round the Earth,
Searching for the Christchild's birth,
And gifts I brought for Him to see
I give to children, secretly.

The Christmas Story

Long ago, in the land of Judea, which today we call Israel, a nation waited for the Saviour prophesied by the Scriptures. This Saviour, everyone believed, would rid the country of the Romans who had conquered Judea and were now the rulers. When the Saviour arrived, they believed, they would be free at last from the taxes and regulations imposed by Rome.

In a quiet area of Judea called Galilee, in the town of Nazareth, lived a young girl called Mary, who was engaged to a local carpenter called Joseph.

One day, when Mary was alone, an angel appeared to her and gave her some amazing news.

"You are to be greatly honoured, Mary," the angel said. "You are to have a son, who will not only rule over this land, but whose kingdom will know no end."

Mary could hardly believe what she was hearing. An ordinary girl like herself to be the mother of the long-awaited Saviour!

An angel had appeared to Joseph, too, and together they waited for the birth of this important baby. But just before the birth was due, the Roman governor of Judea, Caesar Augustus, sent out an order, compelling

everyone to return to his family town to be counted in a census.

Joseph belonged to the family of David, which was at Bethlehem. And so he had to go there, and Mary went with him. They loaded up their donkey and set off.

It was a tiring journey, and because Mary's baby was due soon they could not travel very fast. So they were among the last to arrive in Bethlehem, which was teeming with people who had arrived for the census.

"Don't worry, Mary," said Joseph. "I'll soon find somewhere to stay."

But all the rooms were taken. At last, a kindly innkeeper allowed them to stay in his stable.

"I can't turn my animals out," he said. "But if you don't mind sharing with them, you can sleep there. At least it will be dry and warm."

Joseph prepared the humble stable as best he could. By now, Mary knew that the baby would soon be born, and so Joseph piled sweet-smelling hay into a bed for her, and lined the animals' manger with it as a bed for the baby. When Jesus was born that night, he was tightly wrapped in bands of cloth, as was the custom, and laid in the manger.

Outside, in the night sky, a brilliant new star shone brightly, directly over the stable.

That very same night, in some fields on the outskirts of Bethlehem, a group of shepherds were keeping watch over their flocks of sheep. It is easy to imagine what their conversation must have been about.

"Nice to get away to these fields for some peace and quiet," said one.

"What a turmoil our town is in!"

"That's true, indeed," said another. "All these strangers everywhere! Why, you can hardly move in your own street."

"At least you have your homes to yourselves," retorted another. "I have all my cousins staying with me. There is scarcely room to turn round."

Suddenly the night sky was lit up with a strange light, making the shepherds jump and tremble.

"What is it — what's that?" they cried.

"Don't be afraid," a voice said. "I come with good tidings of great joy for everyone. In your little town tonight a Saviour has been born, who is Christ the Lord."

The shepherds stared speechlessly at the vision before them. An angel! Come to them!

"You will find the baby, wrapped in swaddling clothes, and lying in a manger," went on the angel. And then more angels appeared around them, singing joyfully.

When they had gone, and the hillside was once more shrouded in darkness, the shepherds stood silent, dazzled by what had happened.

"Look here," said one of them at last. "We shall have to go and see for ourselves. A Saviour! The sheep are sure to be all right. Come on, let's hurry!"

They found the stable, and gazed in wonder on the newborn child. Then they rushed away to tell everyone about the visitation from the angels, although it is unlikely that many people believed them.

But Mary did — and many times over the years ahead she was to think about it.

In lands far to the East of Judea, wise men who studied the heavens knew that something marvellous had happened. A new star in the skies always meant that there was an event of importance happening somewhere!

Some of the wise men consulted their books and found that the new star meant that a king had been born. It had to be an important king, and so three of them set out on a pilgrimage, hoping that the star would lead them to the new king.

They were not wrong. The star led them to Judea — and then the wise men began to have doubts. Judea already had a king — Herod! And he was far from new.

"We must visit Herod, and ask him about this new king," said one. So they presented themselves at the door of King Herod's palace.

Herod was greatly disturbed to hear that a new king had been born, but he did not let the wise men see that he was worried. He kept them waiting while he had a secret meeting with all his chief priests and advisors. They were just as worried as he was at the thought of a new king. They all had their comfortable places in the ruling class; under a new king, they might not be so secure!

After the meeting, Herod felt sure of one thing: the new king must have been born in Bethlehem, for his chief priest had reminded him that it was ordained in the Scriptures that a ruler should come from there.

"When you have found the new king, please come back and tell me where he may be found, so that I may worship him, too," he told the wise men. Then he directed them to Bethlehem.

So it was that the wise men joyfully arrived at their journey's end, with the star shining brightly above them, and the stable before them, with the baby and his parents inside.

The wise men fell to their knees in adoration when they saw the child, and offered their gifts to him. What gifts they were, too! There was gold, always a costly gift; and frankincense, one of the most expensive perfumes. Lastly, there was myrrh, richly scented and highly valued.

When the wise men left the stable they thought about what Herod had said. And it seemed as if an angel was warning them to avoid him. So instead of going back to his palace to tell him about the new baby, they journeyed home by another route.

Christmas in Other Lands

Christmas Presents

Father Christmas travels about the sky in a sleigh drawn by reindeer, and he comes down the chimney to leave presents in your stocking. That's right, isn't it?

Lots of children all over Britain shout 'Yes!' but children in other countries could well be shouting 'No!' because Father Christmas can be very different from that. One thing's for sure, though; all good children love him and look forward to the presents he brings, wherever he may live!

Russian children call him Grandfather Frost, and Chinese youngsters know him as Nice Old Father or Christmas Old Man. Americans call him Santa Claus — just as we do, sometimes.

When you hang up your stocking, think of all the other children doing the same thing, or something like it.

It's not always a stocking that gets left for Father Christmas to fill. In France and Holland shoes — or clogs — are left out by the hearth. Spanish children put their shoes on the balcony, to save him coming inside.

Which would you rather hang up? A stocking seems to be a much better thing than any shoe. Even a Wellington boot couldn't hold as much as a nice stretchy stocking!

Present-time isn't always on Christmas Eve and Christmas Day. Right at the start of the Christmas season, on December 6th, Hungarian children put their boots on the windowsills in the hope of finding that St. Nicholas has filled them with presents, next day. This is his feast day, and everyone is on his best behaviour for weeks before that. Is it any wonder — naughty children have been known to find a birch rod instead of a gift!

When Christmas is nearly over, there is still a special treat left for Italian children to look forward to. January 6th is Twelfth Night, and this is the night when the three wise men are believed to have arrived to see the infant Jesus. Just as the wise men brought gifts on that night, so does Befana, spirit of the Epiphany, in Italy. It must be great fun to have a last fling of fun when all the decorations come down. Maybe you could wrap up a few small things for your family on Twelfth Night, and start the custom in your own home? It could be just a small thing, like an orange, a sweet, a picture you have drawn yourself; just something to round off Christmas with a nice surprise all round.

Out and About Together

It seems that everyone likes to join in a procession — for Christmas celebrations often include them!

Swiss children dress up in long white nightshirts, false beards and party hats, and go from house to house in search of gifts. Italian children also go round the houses, reciting Christmas poems for money. There is even more of a ritual in Alaska, where it is so cold that you would think no one would want to venture out at all. Carol-singers carry a huge star with them, as well as many bright lanterns on poles. After Christmas, if they continue to do this, the whole thing becomes a game. Other children, and grown-ups too, are allowed to chase them, in the hope of capturing the star. This represents the hunt by Herod's soldiers to find the Infant Jesus.

One of the strangest processions at Christmas is in Austria. Fruit growers walk around their orchards, tapping all the fruit trees on the trunk and ordering them to bear good fruit the following year. Who knows if it does any good? Better to be on the safe side, the growers must think, as they trail around their muddy land.

Another Austrian custom is for the head of a family to carry a pan of burning charcoal from room to room, followed by all his family. When each room has been entered and the letters C-B-M scrawled in chalk on the doors in memory of the three wise men, Caspar, Balthazar and Melchior, then the house is free of all evil spirits over Christmas.

That custom must certainly date back to pagan times, with the letters an afterthought during the changeover to Christianity. Not that it makes any difference to the fun of Christmas. It's not for reasons of witchcraft or heathen beliefs that these things are still done — but simply because they have been a part of Christmas for so long that it would be a shame to leave them out.

Christmas in Bethlehem

What happens in Bethlehem on Christmas Night nowadays?

There's no census for the people to fill in, but just like Joseph and Mary, if you haven't booked you could find it hard to get lodgings. Thousands of people want to be in Bethlehem for Christmas, just to see what it's like.

There's a church on the spot where, it is said, Jesus was born. It is a Christian church, although Israel is not a Christian land. Three different versions of Christianity share this place of worship, which is called the Church of the Nativity: Roman Catholic, Greek Orthodox and Armenian. Outside the church on Christmas Eve, while Midnight Mass is being celebrated, many people who could not get in worship too. They come from all nations, for Christmas is for anyone who wants it, anywhere in the world.

Spider's Web

There are legends about all kinds of things at Christmas — and as you'll see by the poem below, there is even one about spiders. They had their part to play in the Christmas story, so the legend goes, when they hid the Holy Family from the armies of Herod, who wanted to kill them.

Joseph, Joseph, don't stay any longer,
Take your little family and ride away,
Herod's sending soldiers to search for baby Jesus,
He's jealous and he's powerful, so please don't stay.

Mary, Mary, do not try to argue,
Pack up all your things at once and leave this town,
Get away to Egypt, Herod will not look there,
You can live in safety till the fuss dies down.

Soldiers, soldiers, nearly catching up now!
Who can help that baby, not so far ahead?
Quick now, here's a cavern, tucked into the hillside,
Will the soldiers see it, guess where they have fled?

Spiders, spiders, start your busy spinning,
Weave a lacy curtain at the entrance in the rock,
Soldiers will ride past it, Jesus will be safe now,
And nevermore will anyone the humble spider mock.

The Twelve Days of Christmas

Christmas really lasts for twelve days from December 25 to January 6 which is Epiphany, the day on which we celebrate the arrival of the wise men in Bethlehem. Presents were sometimes given throughout this Christmas period and one of our carols celebrates this with some extraordinary gifts.

On the first day of Christmas
My true love sent to me
A partridge in a pear tree

On the second day of Christmas
My true love sent to me
Two turtle doves
and a partridge in a pear tree

Third day
Three French hens
etc

Fourth day
Four calling birds
etc

Fifth day
Five gold rings
etc

Sixth day
Six geese a-laying
etc

Seventh day
Seven swans a-swimming
etc

Eighth day
Eight maids a-milking
etc

Ninth day
Nine drummers drumming
etc

Tenth day
Ten pipers piping
etc

Eleventh day
Eleven ladies dancing
etc

Twelfth day
Twelve lords a-leaping
etc

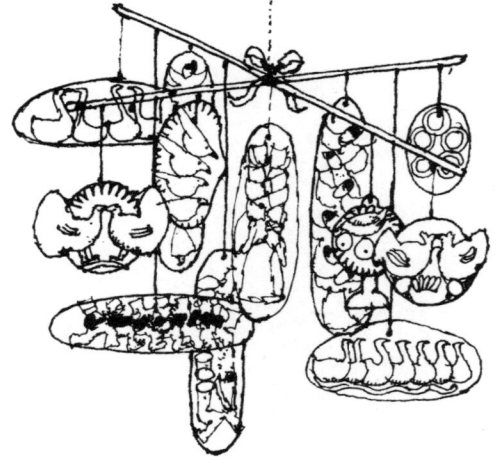

Make a Mobile

Make a beautiful mobile of The Twelve Days of Christmas. All the pieces are on the next pages.

You will need:
Scissors
A metal coat hanger or two small garden canes
Sewing thread
A needle
A cork
Coloured pencils or felt tip pens

1 Cut out all twelve pieces.
2 Colour them in carefully.
3 Make a hole in the top of each piece by pushing a needle through, while you hold a cork underneath.
4 Thread a length of thread through and knot securely.
5 Suspend all the pieces from a coat hanger, making sure they hang at different heights. You could use some small garden canes instead if you prefer.

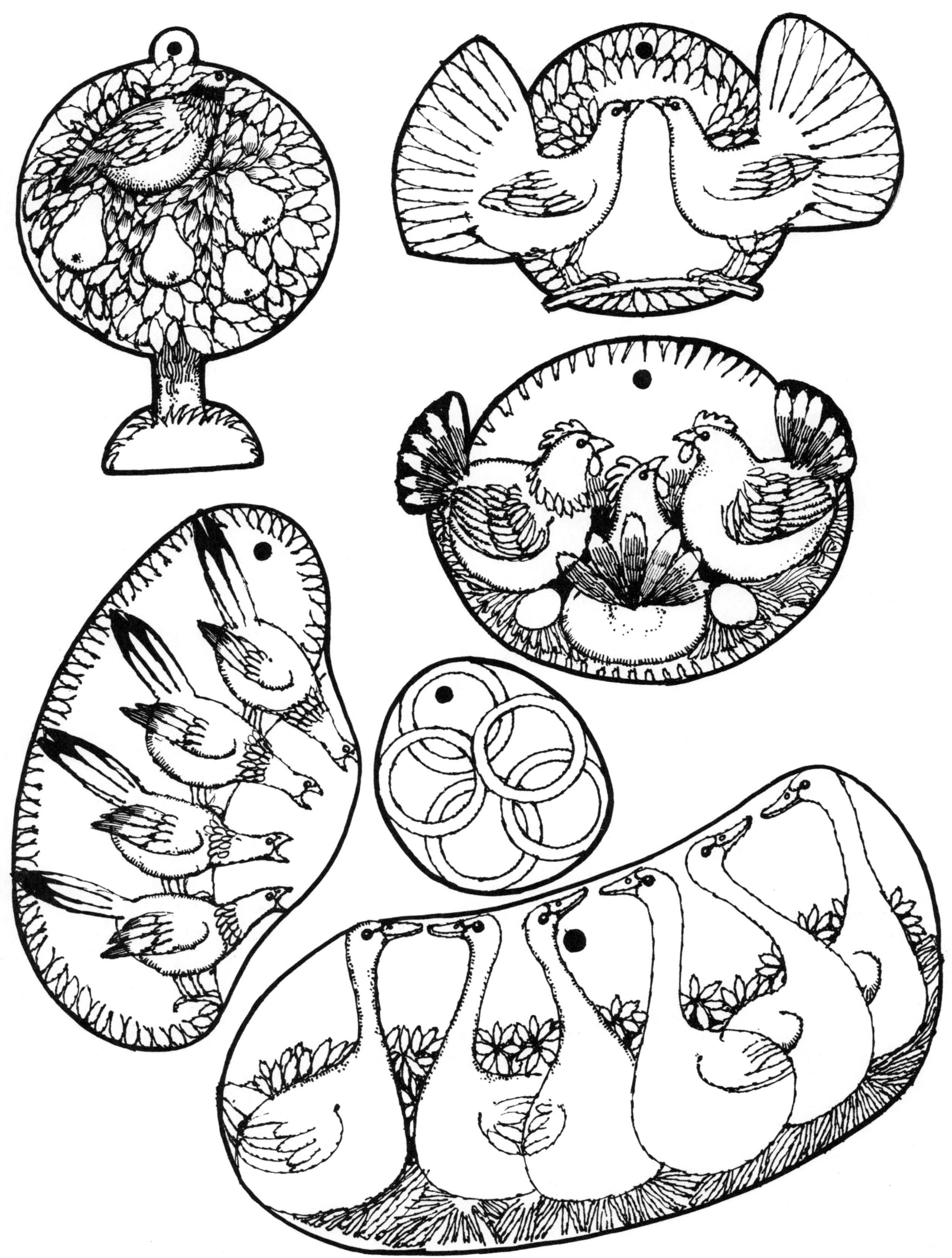

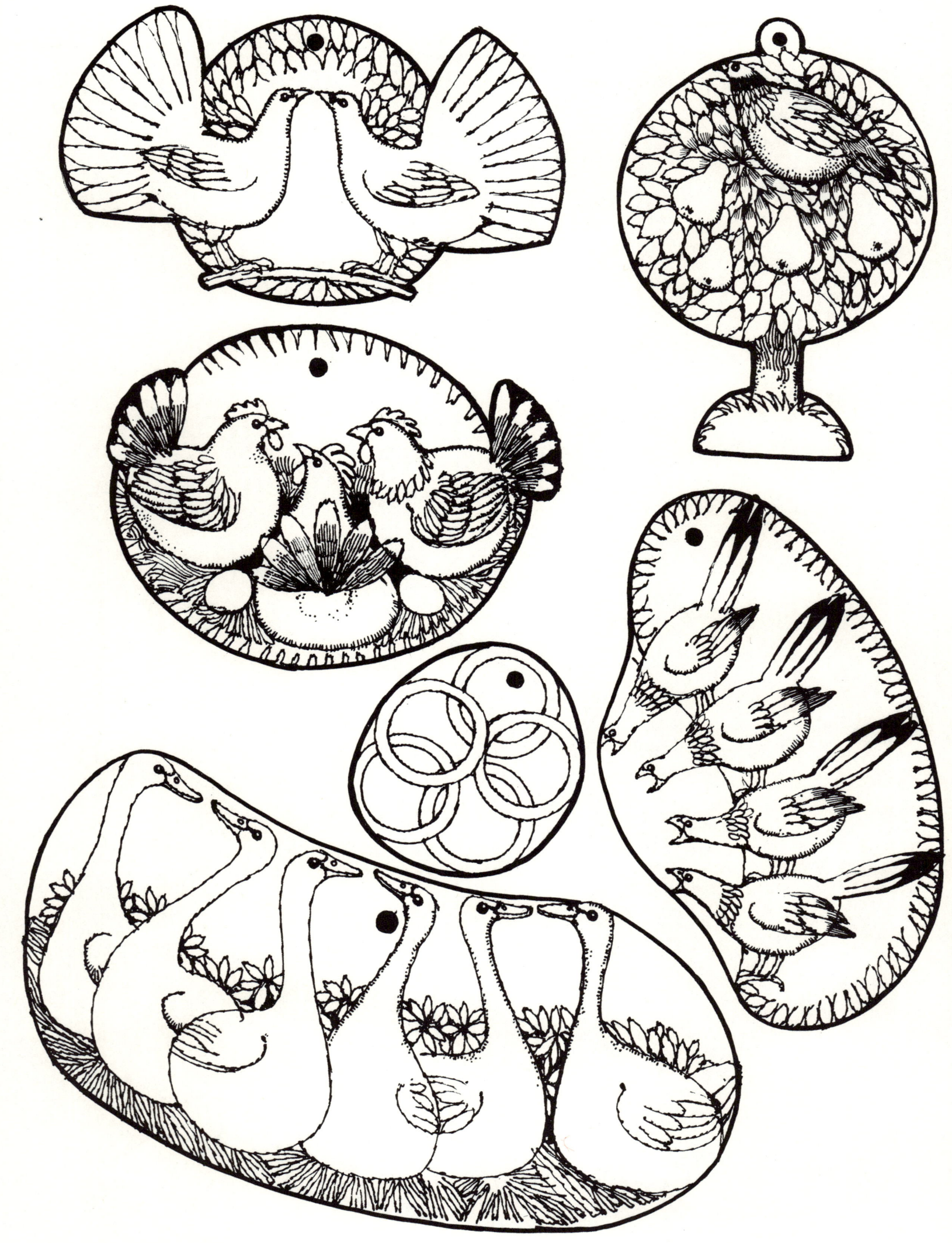

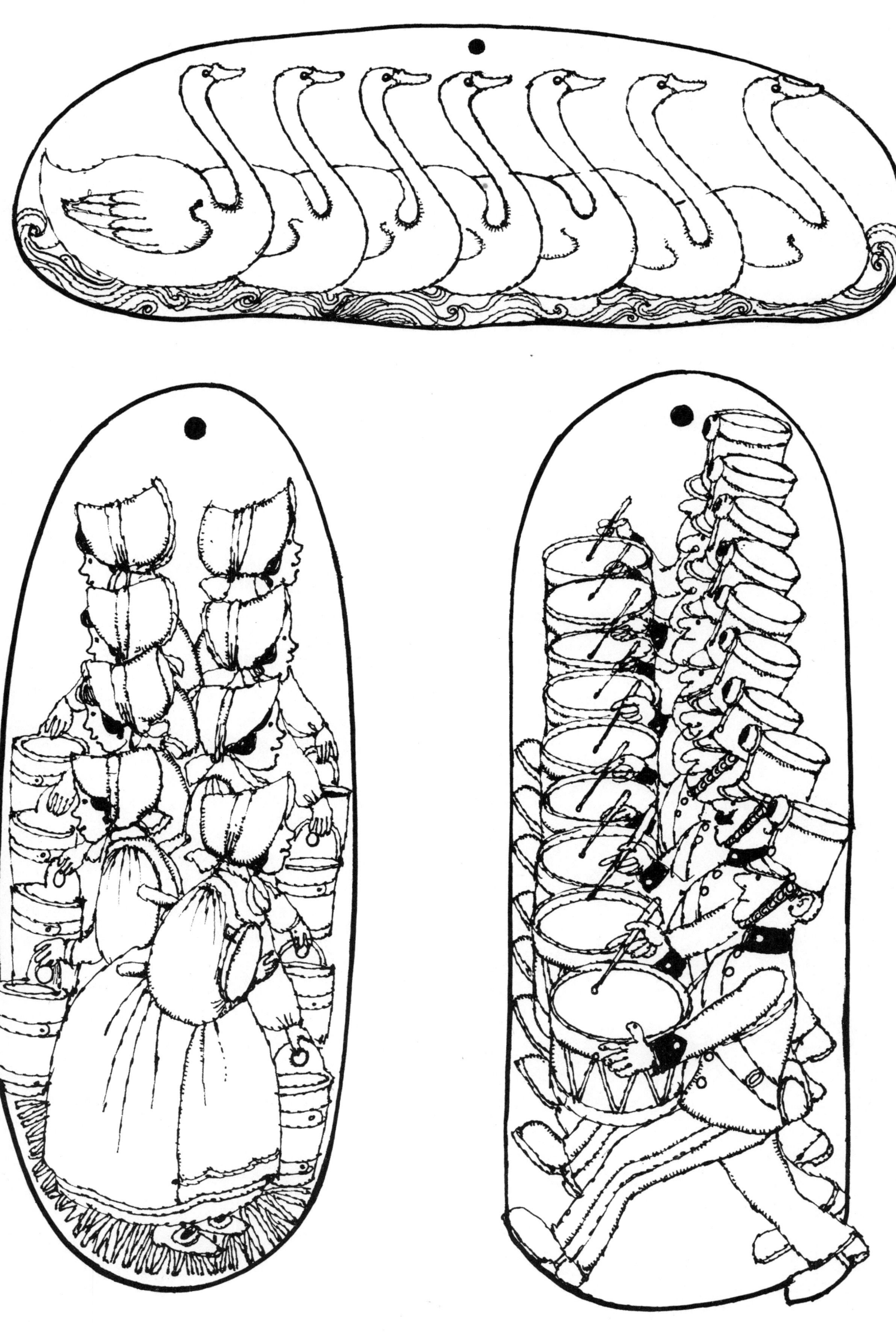

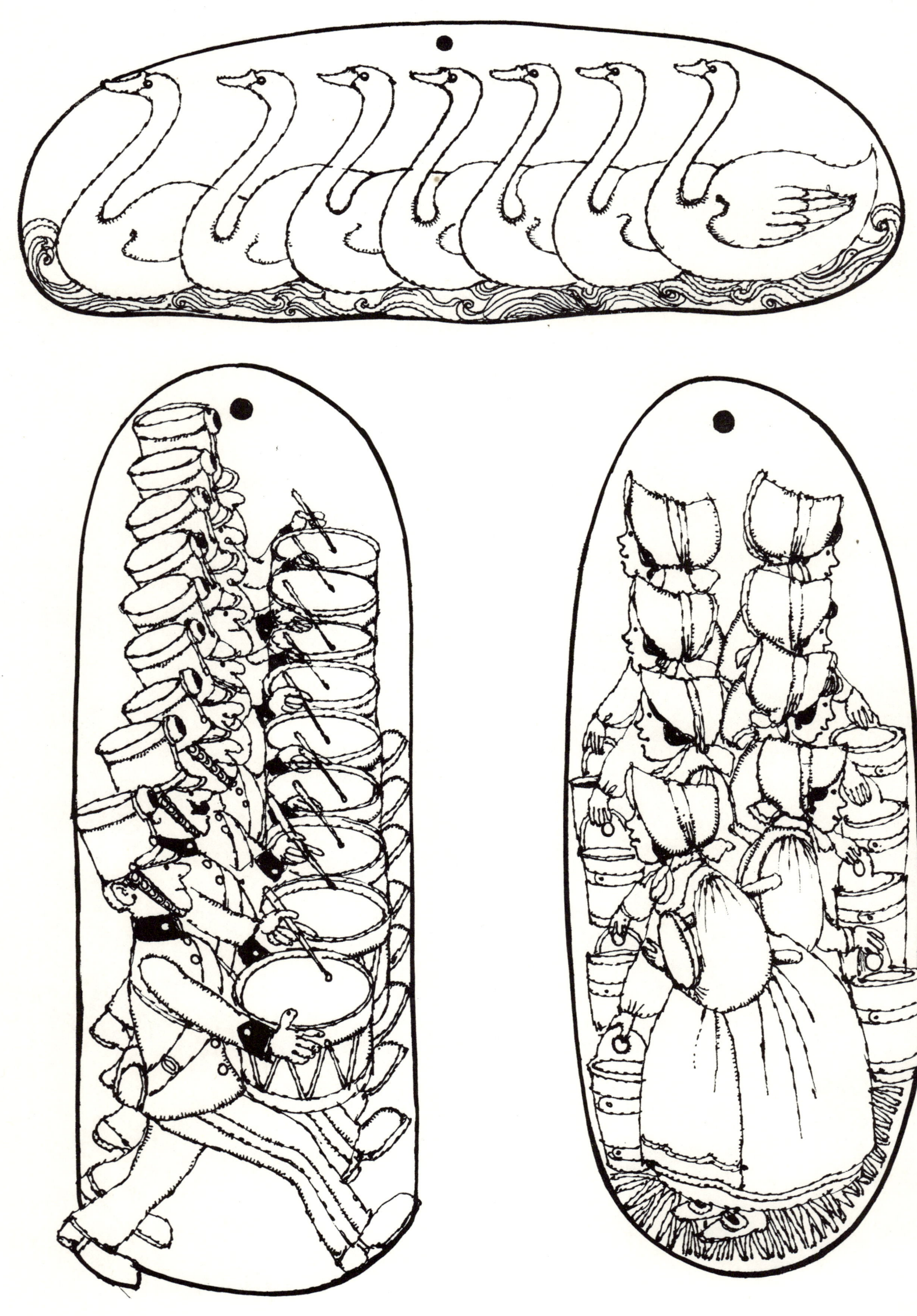

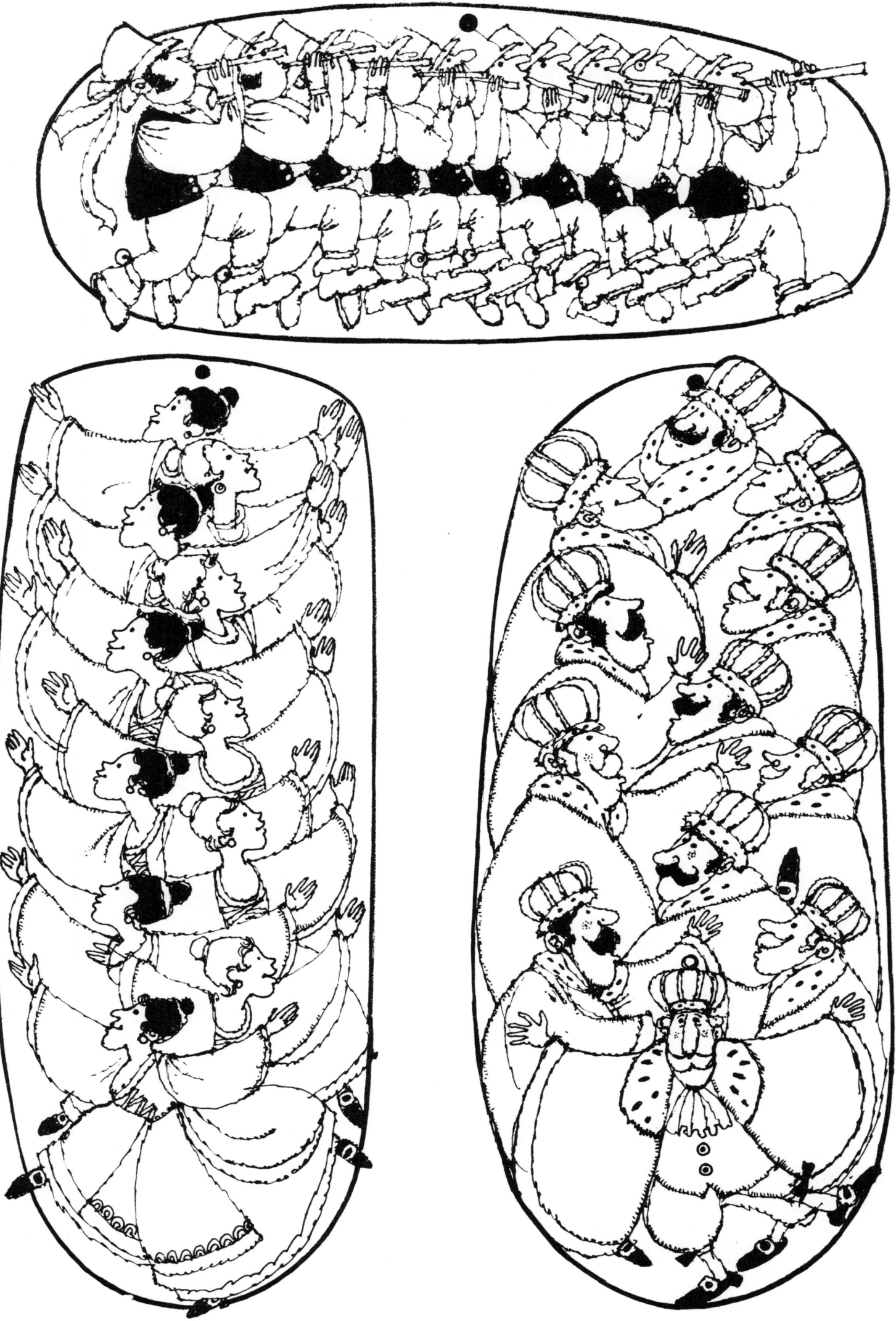

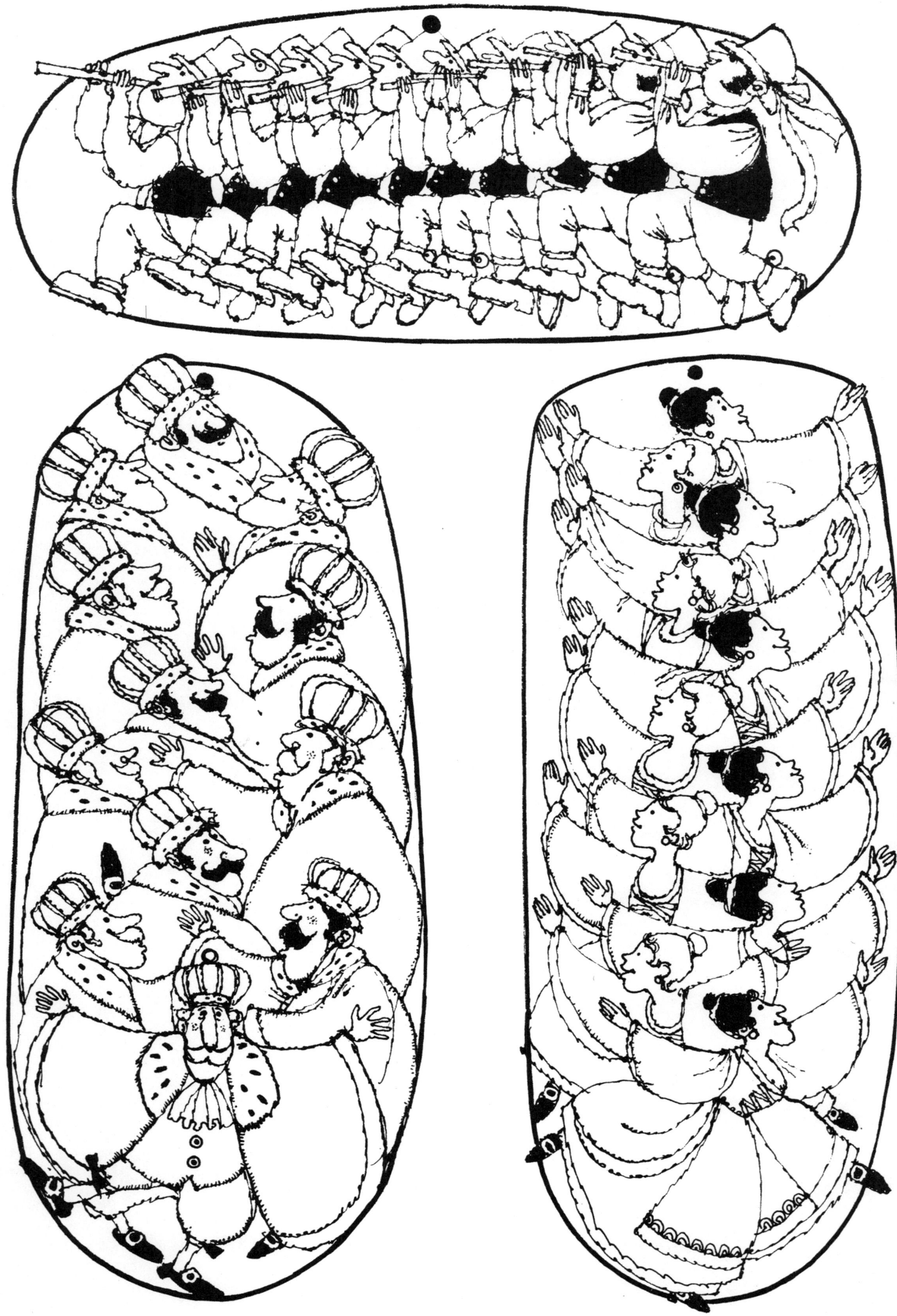